D0131127

Piranhas

A Buddy Book by
Deborah Coldiron

ABDO
Publishing Company

UNDERWATER WORLD

VISIT US AT
www.abdopublishing.com

Published by ABDO Publishing Company, 8000 West 78th Street, Edina, Minnesota 55439.

Copyright © 2009 by Abdo Consulting Group, Inc. International copyrights reserved in all countries. No part of this book may be reproduced in any form without written permission from the publisher. Buddy Books™ is a trademark and logo of ABDO Publishing Company.

Printed in the United States.

Coordinating Series Editor: Sarah Tieck
Contributing Editor: Michael P. Goecke
Graphic Design: Deborah Coldiron
Cover Photograph: Photos.com
Interior Photographs/Illustrations: Animals Animals - Earth Scenes: Chris Catton/Survival/ OSF (page 21), M. Gibbs/OSF (pages 15, 19); Clipart.com (page 11); DK Images (page 19); GeoAtlas (page 9); iStockphoto: Brasil2 (pages 22, 23); Minden Pictures: Claus Meyer (page 13), Flip Nicklin (page 22), Konrad Wothe (page 23); Photos.com (pages 5, 7, 23, 25); Wikipedia.org - Wikipedia Commons: Robyn Broyles (page 23), Grook Da Oger (pages 18, 30), Jonas Hansel (page 17), Omnitarian (page 18), Serefo (page 28), Tino Strauss (page 13), Torox (page 27), R. Wampers (page 19)

Library of Congress Cataloging-in-Publication Data

Coldiron, Deborah.
  Piranhas / Deborah Coldiron.
     p. cm. -- (Underwater world)
  Includes index.
  ISBN 978-1-60453-136-7
  1. Piranhas--Juvenile literature. I. Title.

    QL638.C5C74 2009
    597'.48--dc22
                                                              2008005050

Table Of Contents

The World Of Piranhas 4

A Closer Look 10

A Growing Piranha 14

Family Connections 18

Feeding Frenzy 20

The Amazon Neighborhood . . . 22

A World Of Danger 24

Fascinating Facts 28

Learn And Explore 30

Important Words 31

Web Sites 31

Index 32

The World Of Piranhas

Every living creature needs water. Some animals not only need water, they live in it, too.

Scientists have found more than 250,000 kinds of plants and animals living underwater. And, they believe there could be one million more! The piranha is one animal that makes its home in this underwater world.

Water covers 70 percent of Earth's surface.

Piranhas are native to South America. These freshwater fish are famous for their numerous sharp teeth.

Adult piranhas range from six inches (15 cm) to 24 inches (61 cm) in length. They travel in large groups called schools. And sometimes, these schools attack other animals.

Piranhas have pointed, triangular teeth.

There are about 25 piranha **species** in the world. They flourish in South America's warm rivers and lakes.

Piranhas are now found in Central and North America. Some have even been seen in Hawaii!

Orinoco River

Amazon River

A m a z o n
R i v e r
B a s i n

South
America

Most piranhas live in South
America's Amazon and
Orinoco rivers.

A Closer Look

A piranha has a large, round head. Its strong jaws and many teeth help it tear flesh from prey.

A piranha has many fins that help it control movement. Gill flaps protect the gills.

Large eyes give the piranha good close-up vision and a wide field of vision. This allows the fish to become aware of dangers early.

FAST FACTS A piranha grows replacement teeth throughout its lifetime.

The Body Of A Piranha

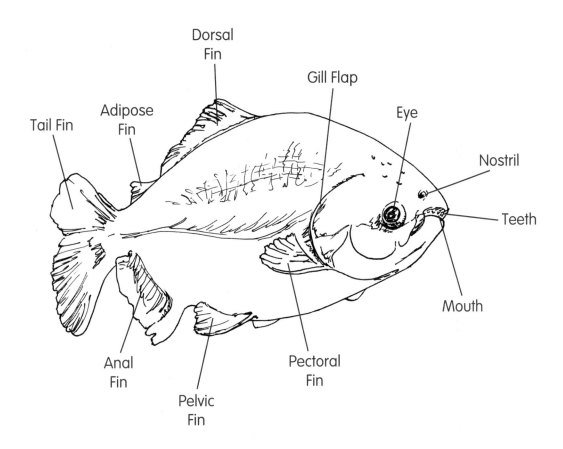

Dorsal Fin

Gill Flap

Adipose Fin

Tail Fin

Eye

Nostril

Teeth

Mouth

Anal Fin

Pelvic Fin

Pectoral Fin

Piranhas vary in size and color. But, many have orange to red bellies and dark-colored fins. Their backs may be white, yellow, green, blue, gray, or black.

Some piranhas have pale, silvery skin. Others sport bright colors or patterns.

A Growing Piranha

When piranhas are ready to **spawn**, they build nests on the river bottom. The female can lay thousands of eggs at one time. After she has finished, the male **fertilizes** them.

Both parents wait for the eggs to hatch. They guard their nest until the young fish are ready to leave.

FAST FACTS

When piranhas are ready to spawn, their bodies change color.

Young piranhas may be covered in stripes or spots. But over time, most piranhas lose these patterns.

After young piranhas leave the nest, they hide among underwater plants. There, they grow about two inches (5 cm) in length. Then, they begin forming large schools with other young piranhas.

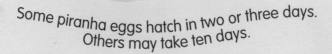

Some piranha eggs hatch in two or three days. Others may take ten days.

Serrasalmus manueli piranhas are also called green tiger piranhas. When they are young, they have green stripes along their sides.

Family Connections

Piranhas belong to a group that includes about 60 **species** of fish. Besides piranhas the group includes pacus and silver-dollar fish.

The red-bellied piranha is the most well-known piranha. This species has the largest teeth and the strongest jaws of all piranha species. And, adult red-bellied piranhas have red eyes.

Pacus have squared-off teeth, much like human teeth. Their strong teeth and jaws are perfect for grinding down hard seeds. So, pacus mainly feed on plants and seeds.

The silver-scaled piranha lives in South America's Tocantins River basin. It is eight inches (20 cm) long. And, it is not considered a danger to humans.

Silver-dollar fish are round, flat fish with silvery bodies. These popular aquarium fish can grow to about five inches (13 cm) in length.

One of the largest piranha species is the San Francisco piranha. It is found in South America's São Francisco River.

Feeding Frenzy

    Piranhas are famous for eating meat. But, their diet includes plants, too.

    Piranhas eat worms, insects, birds, lizards, rodents, snails, and small fish. Some feed on dead animals. And, many eat a variety of plants and seeds.

During a feeding frenzy, piranhas move very quickly and fight for food. Some people say it looks like the water is boiling.

Piranhas travel in schools and share available food. But when food is limited, **feeding frenzies** can occur.

The Amazon Neighborhood

The Amazon River is one of the world's largest river systems. It is about 4,000 miles (6,400 km) long. And, it is home to numerous interesting creatures.

At least 20 different piranha **species** live in the Amazon River. More are found here than in any other river in the world!

Botos are the largest freshwater dolphins in the world. These Amazon river dolphins are one of the piranha's most feared enemies.

Pirarucu are huge freshwater fish. These giants can be 10 feet (3 m) long. And, they can weigh more than 400 pounds (180 kg)!

Anacondas are the heaviest snakes in the world. They live in the Amazon River and surrounding swamps. Most are about 16 feet (5 m) long, but some grow to 30 feet (9 m)!

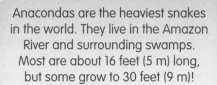

Caimans are similar to alligators. Those found in the Amazon River can be 6 feet (2 m) long! Caimans are strong swimmers and often eat piranhas.

Manatees are plant-eating freshwater animals. Amazonian manatees grow to 10 feet long (3 m). They weigh about 1,000 pounds (450 kg)!

Giant river otters grow to be about 6 feet (2 m) long. These freshwater carnivores love to eat piranhas.

A World Of Danger

Piranhas are food for botos, turtles, birds, giant river otters, and water snakes. Many people eat piranhas, too.

Black caimans prey on piranhas.

South American sport fishermen enjoy catching piranhas. When hooked on a line, they put up a fight. But, their sharp teeth could easily cut a fisherman's line.

Fishermen must take care when handling piranhas. They can deliver powerful bites.

Fascinating Facts

🐟 The name *piranha* comes from two Portuguese words. *Piro* means "fish," and *sainha* means "tooth."

A piranha jaw

Scientists say humans have little to fear from piranhas. When piranhas attack people, there is usually just a single bite. So, scientists believe the person got too close to a piranha nest.

Some aquarium owners have released unwanted piranhas into the wild. This can upset natural pond and river **ecosystems**. So in some parts of the United States, it is illegal to keep pet piranhas.

Learn And Explore

   Professor Anne Magurran is studying why piranhas swim in groups. Scientists thought piranhas formed schools for hunting. But, Professor Magurran's research shows piranhas also form groups for protection.

Forming schools helps piranhas defend against predators.

IMPORTANT WORDS

ecosystem a community of organisms and their surroundings.

feeding frenzy violent feeding by many animals.

fertilize to make fertile. Something that is fertile is capable of growing or developing.

spawn to produce eggs.

species living things that are very much alike.

WEB SITES

To learn more about piranhas, visit ABDO Publishing Company on the World Wide Web. Web sites about piranhas are featured on our Book Links page. These links are routinely monitored and updated to provide the most current information available.

www.abdopublishing.com

INDEX

Amazon River **9, 22, 23**

belly **12**

Central America **8**

color **12, 13, 14, 15, 17, 18, 19**

eggs **14, 16**

enemies **22, 23, 24, 25, 26, 27, 30**

eyes **10, 11, 18**

fins **10, 11, 12**

food **20, 21**

gill flap **10, 11**

green tiger piranha **17**

habitat **4, 6, 8, 9, 14, 16, 19, 22, 29**

head **10**

jaws **10, 18, 28**

life cycle **14, 15, 16, 17**

Magurran, Anne **30**

North America **8, 29**

nostril **11**

Orinoco River **9**

red-bellied piranha **18**

Sans Francisco piranha **19**

São Francisco River **19**

schools **6, 16, 21, 30**

silver-scaled piranha **19**

size **6, 12, 16, 19**

South America **6, 8, 9, 19, 26**

teeth **6, 7, 10, 11, 18, 26**

Tocantins River **19**